READ and SPEAK

JAPANESE

Language Pack for Beginners

by Helen Bagley

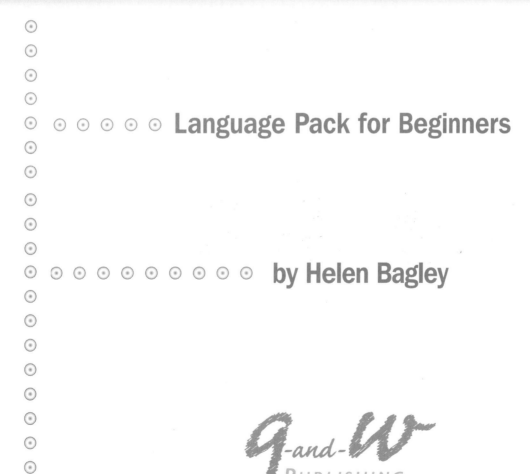

g-and-W
PUBLISHING

Published by g-and-w PUBLISHING
47a High Street
Chinnor
Oxfordshire OX39 4DJ

First published 2004

© g-and-w PUBLISHING 2004

ISBN 1-903103-15-0

Designed by: Mark Wightwick

Illustrated by: Leila Gaafar

Printed in China
by WKT Co. Ltd.

1 2 3 4 5 6 7 8 9   11 10 09 08 07 06 05 04

✳ *plus...*

8 tear-out cards for fun games

Audio CD to enhance your learning

INTRODUCTION

Welcome to *Read and Speak Japanese.* This programme will introduce you to the Japanese language in easy-to-follow steps.

The focus is on enjoyment and understanding, on *reading* words rather than writing them yourself. Through activities and games you'll learn how to read and speak basic Japanese in less time than you thought possible.

You'll find these features in your programme:

Key Words	see them written and hear them on the CD to improve your pronunciation
Language Focuses	clear, simple explanations of language points to help you build up phrases for yourself
Activities	practise what you have learnt in reading, listening, and speaking activities
Games	with tear-out components. Challenge yourself or play with a friend. A great, fun way to review
Audio CD	hear the key words and phrases and take part in interactive listening and speaking activities. You'll find the track numbers next to the activities in your book

If you want to give yourself extra confidence with reading the script, you will find *The Japanese 100 Word Exercise Book* the ideal pre-course companion to this programme. *The Japanese 100 Word Exercise Book* introduces the Japanese script through 100 key everyday words, many of which also feature in *Read and Speak Japanese.*

So now you can take your first steps in Japanese with confidence, enjoyment, and a real sense of progress.

Whenever you see the audio CD symbol, you'll find listening and speaking activities on the CD included with this book. The symbol shows the track number.

Track 1 is an introduction to the sounds of Japanese. Listen to this before you start and come back to it again at later stages if you need to.

Key Words

Look at the script for each key word and try to visualize it, connecting its image to the pronunciation you hear on your CD.

こんにちは　*hello*　Japanese names:

konnichiwa

安紀子 **akiko** *(female)*

さようなら　*goodbye*

優子 **yuuko** *(female)*

sayounara

正 **tadashi** *(male)*

... です　... **desu**　*I am ...*

実 **minoru** *(male)*

⊙ *Japanese is written in a combination of three writing systems –*
⊙ *hiragana and katakana alphabets, or "syllabaries", and Chinese*
⊙ *characters, known as kanji. For example, the greetings in the left-hand*
⊙ *column above are written in hiragana, but the names on the right are*
⊙ *written in kanji. How a particular word is written depends on the origin*
⊙ *of the word and convention.*

⊙ *You will find an overview of the script, including hiragana and katakana*
⊙ *tables, in the reference section on page 89, but don't expect to take it all in*
⊙ *at once. Concentrate only on the hiragana you need for the three phrases*
⊙ *in the Key Words for the moment and build up gradually from there.*

⊙ *Kanji characters offer no clue as to their pronunciation and need to be*
⊙ *learnt one by one. Look carefully at the characters while listening to the*
⊙ *CD, connecting the image to the pronunciation you hear.*

TOPIC 1: What's your name?

How do you say it?

Join the script to the pronunciation, as in the example.

akiko	実
minoru	こんにちは
konnichiwa	優子
yuuko	さようなら
tadashi	です
sayounara	安紀子
desu	正

What does it mean?

Now say the Japanese out loud and write the English next to each.

こんにちは   *hello*   さようなら _____

優子 _____   実 _____

です _____   安紀子 _____

正 _____

Language Focus

⊙ ⊙ ⊙ ⊙ ⊙ To introduce yourself simply say your name, followed by です **desu**.

> 安紀子です。 **akiko desu.** *I'm Akiko.*
>
> 正です。 **tadashi desu.** *I'm Tadashi.*

です **desu** does not change for male or female or the number of people and so also means *he/she <u>is</u>, they <u>are</u>,* etc.

⊙ ⊙ ⊙ ⊙ When you are addressing someone by name in Japanese you need to add the word さん **san** after the person's name. This is the equivalent of Mr., Miss, Mrs., and Ms. and is used with both first and last names. It is used much more than its English equivalents. Never use さん **san** when talking about yourself.

> 実さん、こんにちは。 **minoru san, konnichiwa.**
> *Hello, Minoru.*
>
> 優子さん、さようなら。 **yuuko san, sayounara.**
> *Goodbye, Yuuko.*

⊙ ⊙ ⊙ The period is written as a small circle in Japanese script: 。

⊙ ⊙ You will notice that Japanese does not have spaces between separate words. This can make reading longer sentences tricky. Try to look for words that you recognize. As you progress through this book you will soon realize that there are lots of words that re-occur, like です **desu**. Look out for these words to help you break up the sentences.

TRACK NUMBER
3

⊙
⊙   *Practise introducing yourself and learn some*
⊙   *useful replies on your CD.*
⊙

TOPIC 1: What's your name?

What are they saying?

Write the correct number in the word balloons.

1 こんにちは。安紀子です。
konnichiwa. akiko desu.

2 実さん、こんにちは。
minoru san, konnichiwa.

3 さようなら。 **sayounara.**

4 優子さん、こんにちは。
yuuko san, konnichiwa.

What do you hear?

TRACK NUMBER

4

Work out the phrases below. Then listen and tick (✔) the two phrases you hear on your audio CD.

1 優子さん、さようなら。 ☐

2 正です。 ☐

3 実さん、さようなら。 ☐

4 安紀子さん、こんにちは。 ☐

5 こんにちは。 ☐

TOPIC 1: What's your name?

Key Words

お名前は(何ですか)。 **onamae wa (nan desu ka)?** *what's your name?*

どうぞ。 **douzo** *please*

ありがとうございます。 **arigatou gozaimasu** *thank you*

おはようございます。 **ohayou gozaimasu** *good morning*

こんばんは。 **konban wa** *good evening*

Language Focus

○ ○ ○ ○ ○ The full version of the question *what's your name?* お名前は何ですか **onamae wa nan desu ka?** is formed by combining お名前 **onamae** *(name)* with the question word 何 **nan/nani** *(what?)*, です **desu** *(is)* and the question marker か **ka**. は **wa** is a topic marker and can be roughly translated as *as for*. So literally the question means *"as for name what is it?"*

○ ○ ○ ○ Notice that we can shorten the question to: お名前は？ **onamae wa?** In this case there is no question marker, so it is important to raise your voice at the end of the question. This is less formal than the full version.

○ ○ ○ However, you should be aware that in Japan it is not so common to ask someone's name directly. When meeting someone for the first time you would usually introduce yourself, giving your family name first followed by your first name. The other person would then do the same.

TOPIC 1: What's your name?

Speaking practice

Practise the Japanese you have learnt so far.

TRACK NUMBER
6

What does it mean?

Match the English word balloons to the Japanese.

For example: **1b**

1 *Good morning.*	a どうぞ。
2 *Hello.*	b おはようございます。
3 *What's your name?*	c ありがとうございます。
4 *Please.*	d 正です。
5 *My name's Tadashi.*	e お名前は(何ですか)。
6 *Thank you.*	f こんにちは。

Which word?

Write the correct number of the word in the box to complete the conversation, as in the example.

1 正	2 ございます	3 は
	4 です	5 おはよう

おはよう __2__.

____ございます。

安紀子____。お名前____。

____です。

TOPIC 1: What's your name?

Language Focus

⊙ ⊙ ⊙ ⊙ ⊙ All of the words you have met so far have been written in either *hiragana* or *kanji* (Chinese characters).

⊙ ⊙ ⊙ ⊙ The third writing system is *katakana*. This alphabet, or to be more accurate "syllabary", is used for all borrowed words including foreign names. As a general rule, katakana is squarer and less ornate than hiragana. You'll find a chart for katakana on page 91.

⊙ ⊙ ⊙ English names will be written in katakana but may be spelt slightly differently. Sarah for example is spelt セーラ **seera**. The ー that you see is used to make the previous vowel long, changing セ **se** to セー **see**. Names which include the English letter *l* are written with the letter *r*. So *Helen* becomes ヘレン **heren**.

What are their names?

Can you work out these common English names in Japanese script?
Use the katakana table on page 91 to help you work them out.

セーラ	*seera Sarah*	ピーター	_____
ヘレン	_____	ケン	_____
メリー	_____	マーク	_____
リサ	_____	ロバート	_____
ハナ	_____	ジェームス	_____

ACTIVITY

In or out?

Who is in the office today and who is out at meetings? Look at the wallchart and write the names in English in the correct column, as in the example.

セーラ	✔
実	✔
ジェームス	✘
優子	✔
ロバート	✘
安紀子	✘
ケン	✔
正	✔
ヘレン	✘
メリー	✘

IN　　　　　**OUT**

Sarah

TOPIC 1: What's your name?

The Name Game

1. Tear out Game Card 1 at the back of your book and cut out the name cards (leave the sentence-build cards at the bottom of the sheet for the moment).

2. Put the cards Japanese side up and see if you can recognize the names. Turn over the cards to see if you were correct.

3. Keep shuffling the cards and testing yourself until you can read all the names.

4. Then cut out the extra sentence-build cards at the bottom of the sheet and make mini-dialogues. For example:

   – **konban wa. onamae wa?**

   – **heren desu.**

5. You can also play with a friend. Make mini-dialogues for each other to read. If you both have a book, you can play pairs (pelmanism) with both sets of cards, saying the words as you turn over the cards.

TOPIC 1: What's your name?

Key Words

日本 **nihon/nippon** *Japan*

中国 **chuugoku** *China*

韓国 **kankoku** *Korea*

アメリカ **amerika** *America*

イギリス **igirisu** *England*

カナダ **kanada** *Canada*

アイルランド **airurando** *Ireland*

オーストラリア **oosutoraria** *Australia*

国 **kuni** *country*

市 **shi** *city*

Notice how Japan *and other countries in the region are written in kanji, but Western country names, such as* America, *are written phonetically in katakana.*

To learn new words, try covering the English and looking at the Japanese script and pronunciation. Start from the first word and work your way to the last word seeing if you can remember the English. Then do the same but this time starting from the bottom and moving up to the first word. See if you can go down and up three times without making any mistakes. Then try looking only at the Japanese characters and see if you can remember the pronunciation and meaning. When you can recognize all the words, cover the Japanese and this time look at the English saying the Japanese out loud.

Where are the countries?

Write the number next to the country, as in the example.

カナダ _1_   イギリス __   日本 __   オーストラリア __

韓国 __   アイルランド __   アメリカ __   中国 __

TOPIC 2: Where are you from?

How do you say it?

Join the English to the pronunciation and the Japanese script, as in the example.

England	**kuni**	中国
Korea	**igirisu**	オーストラリア
Ireland	**kanada**	国
city	**kankoku**	アイルランド
China	**shi**	市
Canada	**airurando**	イギリス
America	**oosutoraria**	韓国
country	**nihon/nippon**	アメリカ
Australia	**chuugoku**	日本
Japan	**amerika**	カナダ

Where are the cities?

Now look at these cities and make sentences like this, using the phrase にあります **ni arimasu:**

東京は日本にあります。 **toukyou wa nihon ni arimasu.** *Tokyo is in Japan.*

Tokyo	*New York*	*Washington*	*Los Angeles*
東京	ニューヨーク	ワシントン	ロサンジェルス
toukyou	**nyuuyooku**	**washinton**	**rosanjerusu**

Osaka	*Sydney*	*London*	*Dublin*
大阪	シドニー	ロンドン	ダブリン
oosaka	**shidonii**	**rondon**	**daburin**

TOPIC 2: Where are you from?

Language Focus

When talking about where we come from in Japanese it is more common to refer to our nationality. This is very simple to do. Simply add the word for *person,* 人 **jin,** to the country, followed by です **desu** *(I am)*.

> アメリカ人です。　**amerikajin desu.** *I'm American.*
>
> 日本人です。　**nihonjin desu.** *I'm Japanese.*

If you wish to specify the town or city you come from you would use the formula *town/city* + から来ました **kara kimashita.** から **kara** meaning *from* and 来ました **kimashita** meaning *have come*. You can say what town/city and what country you come from in the same sentence linking them with の **no** *("of")*:

> イギリスのロンドンから来ました。
> **igirisu no rondon kara kimashita.**
> *I'm from London in England.*

To ask the question *What nationality are you?* the word order is:
何 **nan/nani** *(what)* + 人 **jin** *(person)* + です **desu** + か **ka** *(question marker)*

> 何人ですか。　**nani jin desu ka?** *What nationality are you?*
>
> イギリス人です。　**igirisujin desu.** *I'm English.*

You can use どこ **doko** *(where?)* to ask someone what town/city they are from:

> どこから来ましたか。　**doko kara kimashita ka?**
> *Where are you from?*
>
> 大阪から来ました。　**oosaka kara kimashita.**
> *I'm from Osaka.*

TRACK NUMBER
8

⊙　*Listen to four different people introducing themselves and*
⊙　*see if you can understand where they are from.*

TOPIC 2: Where are you from?

Where are they from?

Join the people to their nationalities, as in the example. Listen again to track 8 on your CD and look back at the names and countries if you need to remind yourself.

安紀子   イギリス

メリー   中国

セーラ   オーストラリア

ケン   日本

Where are you from?

Now say where you're from.
Follow the prompts on your audio CD.

Key Words

人 **jin/hito**   *person*   から **kara**   *from*

何 **nan/nani** *what*   どこ **doko?** *where?*

さん **san**   *Mr./Mrs./Ms./Miss*   か **ka?**   question marker

TOPIC 2: Where are you from?

Language Focus

⊙ ⊙ ⊙ ⊙　English refers to other people as *he* or *she*: *He is American*, *She is from New York*, etc. Japanese speakers rarely use the pronouns for *you*, *he*, *she*, etc. Instead they prefer to use the person's name followed by the title さん **san.**

> 安紀子さんは日本人です。
> **akiko san wa nihonjin desu.**
> *She (Akiko) is Japanese.*
>
> ケンさんは中国のペキンから来ました。
> **ken san wa chuugoku no pekin kara kimashita.**
> *He (Ken) is from Beijing in China.*

⊙ ⊙ ⊙ ⊙　The question 何人ですか。 **nani jin desu ka?** can mean *What nationality are you/he/she/they?* etc. depending on who you are talking to, or about. To make it more specific you would need to use the person's name. Again さん **san** is needed after the name, together with the topic marker は **wa** *("as for")*.

> セーラさんは、何人ですか。
> **seera san wa nani jin desu ka?**
> *Sarah, what nationality are you?* (when talking <u>to</u> Sarah) OR
> *What nationality is Sarah?* (when talking <u>about</u> Sarah)

This makes life very easy, but it does mean that you have to remember people's names!

⊙ ⊙ ⊙　You have probably noticed that the Japanese script doesn't use question marks very much. This is because the question marker か **ka** will indicate that the phrase is a question without the need to use an additional question mark. However if か **ka** is not used, such as in お名前は？ **onamae wa?** then you will usually see a question mark.

TOPIC 2: Where are you from?

Who's from where?

Make questions and answers about where these people are from, as in the example.

1
ピーター

ピーターさんは何人ですか。
piitaa san wa nani jin desu ka?
What nationality is Peter?

ピーターさんはアメリカ人です。
piitaa san wa amerikajin desu.
Peter is American.

2
優子

3
リサ

4
マーク

5
ジェームス

6
スン

7
実

8
メリー

TOPIC 2: Where are you from?

Listen and check

TRACK NUMBER
11

Listen to the conversation on your audio CD and decide if these sentences are true or false.

		True	False
1	The woman's name is Sophie.	☐	☐
2	She comes from Canada.	☐	☐
3	The man's name is Tadashi.	☐	☐
4	He comes from Japan.	☐	☐
5	They are already friends.	☐	☐

What does it mean?

Now read the Japanese you heard in the conversation and match it with English, as in the example.

English	Japanese
I'm from Canada.	はじめまして。
He's from Japan.	カナダ人です。
My name's Lucy.	お名前は？
What's your name?	日本人です。
How do you do?	どうぞよろしく。
Pleased to meet you.	ルーシーです。

I'm from Canada. is matched with カナダ人です。

What does it mean?

Try to work out each of these sentences. It will help if you break them up into the separate words and phrases. Look back at the Key Word panels if you need help.

Then read the sentences out loud when you have worked them out and write the English next to each, as in the example.

1 ルーシーです。   <u>My name is Lucy.</u>

2 カナダ人です。   _____

3 優子さんは日本人です。   _____

4 お名前は？   _____

5 安紀子です。   _____

6 ピーターさんは何人ですか。   _____

7 ジェームスさんはイギリス人です。   _____

8 アメリカ人です。   _____

You can compare your pronunciation of the sentences with the models on your audio CD.

TRACK NUMBER
12

Now complete this description of yourself. Read the sentences out loud, adding your own details.

... です。

... の ... から来ました。

TOPIC 2: Where are you from?

The Flag Game

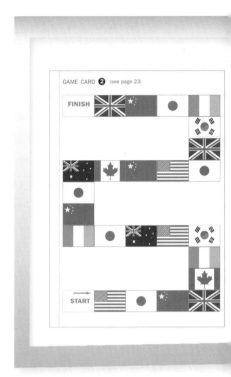

(1) Tear out Game Card 2.

(2) Find a die and counter(s).

(3) Put the counter(s) on START.

(4) Throw the die and move that number of squares.

(5) When you land on a flag, you must ask and answer the appropriate question for that country. For example:

何人ですか。 **nani jin desu ka?**
(What nationality are you?)

イギリス人です。 **igirisujin desu.**
(I'm English.)

(6) If you can't remember the question or answer, you must go back to the square you came from. You must throw the exact number to finish.

(7) You can challenge yourself or play with a friend.

TOPIC 2: Where are you from?

Key Words

椅子 **isu**	*chair*	ドア **doa**		*door*
テーブル **teeberu**	*table*	窓 **mado**		*window*
テレビ **terebi**	*television*	ペン **pen**		*pen*
本 **hon**	*book*	雑誌 **zasshi**		*magazine*
かばん **kaban**	*bag*	ソファー **sofaa**		*sofa*
コンピュータ **konpyuuta**	*computer*	電話 **denwa**		*telephone*

Notice how all three writing systems are represented in the words above.

Original Japanese words are written in either kanji, for example 本 hon (book) *and* 窓 mado (window), *or in hiragana, for example* かばん kaban (bag).

Loan words are written in katakana, for example ソファー sofaa (sofa) *and* テレビ terebi (television).

TOPIC 3: What's this?

Language Focus

⊙ ⊙ ⊙ ⊙ Japanese nouns do not have articles *(a/an, the)*. Plurals are also very simple – there aren't any! So 本 **hon** can mean *book, a book, the book, books,* or *the books.*

What does it mean?

Match the Japanese with the pictures, then write the pronunciation and the English.

ソファー　_____

電話　_____

ドア　_____

窓　*mado* window(s)_____

ペン　_____

かばん　_____

コンピュータ　_____

椅子　_____

テーブル　_____

テレビ　_____

本　_____

雑誌　_____

Word Square

Can you find the 8 key words in the word square? Circle them and write the English, as in the example. The words can be horizontal or vertical.

小	園	ラ	ソ	テ	ー	ブ	ル
か	ば	ん	ス	レ	髪	港	ン
さ	公	で	さ	ビ	園	車	本
お	電	空	よ	タ	フ	ク	す
ご	コ	ン	ピ	ュ	ー	タ	あ
レ	ー	毛	い	腹	テ	ら	そ
ト	雑	誌	う	の	な	椅	こ
ソ	フ	ァ	ー	公	シ	子	シ

computer _____

_____

_____

_____

_____

Odd One Out

Which is the odd one out? Circle the word in each row that doesn't belong.

椅子 ＊ テーブル ＊ お名前 ＊ ソファー

電話 ＊ 日本 ＊ アメリカ ＊ 韓国

安紀子 ＊ ペン ＊ ロバート ＊ セーラ

かばん ＊ こんばんは ＊ さようなら ＊ こんにちは

何 ＊ か ＊ どこ ＊ ドア

TOPIC 3: What's this?

Language Focus

○ ○ ○ ○ ○ We have already met the words for *what*, 何 **nan/nani,** and *is*, です **desu.** Using these we can ask *What is it?/What are they?*:

> 何ですか。 **nan desu ka?** *What is it?/What are they?*
>
> 椅子です。 **isu desu.** *It's a chair./They're chairs.*

○ ○ ○ ○ ○ To ask *What's this?/What's that?* Japanese makes a distinction depending on the position of the object being talked about:

これ **kore** *this thing here*: when the object is near to the speaker

それ **sore** *that thing there*: when the object is nearer to the listener

あれ **are** *that thing over there*: when the object is far away from both listener and speaker

A question asked with これ **kore** would therefore usually be answered using それ **sore** and *vice versa*. Questions asked with あれ **are** are usually answered also using あれ **are**.

> これは何ですか。 → それはテーブルです。
> **kore wa nan desu ka?** **sore wa teeberu desu.**
> *What's this (thing here)?* *That (thing there) is a table.*
>
> あれは何ですか。 → あれはかばんです。
> **are wa nan desu ka?** **are wa kaban desu.**
> *What's that (thing over there)?* *That (thing over there) is a bag.*

○ ○ ○ ○ A *yes/no* question can be answered using either いいえ **iie** *(no)* or the useful phrase はい、そうです **hai, sou desu** *(yes, that's right)*.

> それは本ですか。 **sore wa hon desu ka.** *Is that a book?*
>
> いいえ、これは雑誌です。 はい、そうです。
> **iie, kore wa zasshi desu.** **hai, sou desu.**
> *No, this is a magazine.* *Yes, that's right.*

Your turn to speak

TRACK NUMBER

14

Now ask what things are.
Follow the prompts on your audio CD.

What is it?

Look at the pictures of everyday objects from unusual angles. Then read the sentences and decide which picture they describe, as in the example.

1 椅子です。 *e*

2 コンピュータです。 __

3 ソファーです。 __

4 電話です。 __

5 ドアです。 __

6 テレビです。 __

7 ペンです。 __

8 かばんです。 __

Key Words

紅茶 **koocha**	black tea	サンドイッチ **sandoicchi**	sandwich
お茶 **ocha**	green tea	そば **soba**	noodles
コーヒー **koohii**	coffee	豚カツ **tonkatsu**	pork cutlet
ケーキ **keeki**	cake		

Language Focus

⊙ ⊙ ⊙ ⊙ ⊙ To request an item in Japanese we use the following pattern:
item + をお願いします **o onegaishimasu**:

> コーヒーをお願いします。 **koohii o onegaishimasu.**
> *I'd like a coffee.*

⊙ ⊙ ⊙ ⊙ ⊙ To request more than one item simply link them using と **to** *(and)*:

> コーヒーとサンドイッチをお願いします。
> **koohii to sandoicchi o onegaishimasu.**
> *I'd like a coffee and a sandwich.*

⊙ ⊙ ⊙ Having asked for an item you will hear the word どうぞ **douzo** *(please)* when it is handed to you.

> お茶をどうぞ。 **ocha o douzo.**
> *Here's your green tea. ("green tea, please")*
> ありがとうございます。 **arigatou gozaimasu.**
> *Thank you.*

Who orders what?

What are the customers ordering? Listen to your
CD and check what they order, as in the example.

Note that when you enter a shop or restaurant, etc., you will be welcomed with a
shout of いらっしゃいませ **irasshaimase** (*can I help you?*), rather than *hello*.

	black tea	green tea	coffee	sandwich	cake	noodles	pork cutlet
Customer 1			✓		✓		
Customer 2							
Customer 3							
Customer 4							
Customer 5							

Now look at the table above and pretend you are ordering for yourself.

コーヒーとケーキをお願いします。 **koohii to keeki o onegaishimasu.**

TOPIC 3: What's this?

Unscramble the conversation

Can you put this conversation in the correct order?

ORDER: g, _____

Now check your answer with the conversation on your audio CD.

TOPIC 3: What's this?

At the café

TRACK NUMBER
18

Your turn to order now. Look at the menu below and
then you'll be ready to order from the waiter on your CD.

紅茶

お茶

コーヒー

サンドイッチ

ケーキ

そば

豚カツ

TOPIC 3: What's this?

The Café Game

1. Cut out the picture cards from Game Card 3.

2. Put the cards into a bag.

3. Shake the bag.

4. Pull out a card without looking.

5. Ask for the item on the card. For example:

   お茶をお願いします。

   ocha o onegaishimasu.

   (*I'd like a green tea.*)

6. If you can ask the question out loud quickly and fluently, then put the card aside. If not, then put it back into the bag.

7. See how long it takes you to get all of the cards out of the bag. Or play with a friend and see who can collect the most cards.

TOPIC 3: What's this?

Key Words

TRACK NUMBER

19

部屋 **heya**	*room*	家 **ie**	*house*
冷蔵庫 **reizouko**	*refrigerator*	木 **ki**	*tree*
戸棚 **todana**	*cupboard*	車 **kuruma**	*car*
レンジ **renji**	*stove*	猫 **neko**	*cat*
ベッド **beddo**	*bed*	犬 **inu**	*dog*
絵 **e**	*picture*	ネズミ **nezumi**	*mouse*

Language Focus

⊙ ⊙ ⊙ ⊙ Japanese kanji words can be a single character, such as 犬 **inu** *(dog)* or 車 **kuruma** *(car),* or a combination of two or more characters, such as 部屋 **heya** *(room)* or 冷蔵庫 **reizouko** *(refrigerator)*.

Sometimes you can find common characters, such as 茶 **cha** *(tea)*, which you have met in 紅茶 **koocha** *(black tea)* and お茶 **ocha** *(green tea)*. Looking out for common characters can help you remember kanji.

A word of warning: sometimes the same kanji character is pronounced completely differently in combination. For example, 国 **kuni** *(country)* but 中国 **chuugoku** *(China)*.

TOPIC 4: Where is it?

What does it mean?

Join the Japanese to the pronunciation and write down the meaning in English.

絵	nezumi	_____
部屋	renji	_____
冷蔵庫	ki	_____
木	kuruma	_____
ネズミ	e	*picture*
ベッド	neko	_____
車	todana	_____
猫	ie	_____
戸棚	inu	_____
犬	beddo	_____
レンジ	heya	_____
家	reizouko	_____

What can you see?

Look at the picture and tick (✔) the things you can see, as in the example.

レンジ ✔	ベッド ☐
冷蔵庫 ☐	戸棚 ☐
絵 ☐	木 ☐
コンピュータ ☐	猫 ☐
テーブル ☐	椅子 ☐
車 ☐	本 ☐
窓 ☐	犬 ☐
ペン ☐	かばん ☐
雑誌 ☐	ネズミ ☐

TOPIC 4: Where is it?

Key Words

中 **naka** *in(side)*

上 **ue** *on (top of)/ above*

下 **shita** *under*

前 **mae** *in front of*

後ろ **ushiro** *behind*

となり **tonari** *next to*

TRACK NUMBER
20

Language Focus

To say where something is in English we simply place the preposition (positional word) in the middle of the two objects: *The book is <u>on</u> the table*. In Japanese the preposition comes at the end of the sentence:

本はテーブルの上です。 **hon wa teeburu no ue desu.**
The book is on the table.

As in English the object whose location we are describing comes at the start of the sentence, and is marked by the topic marker は **wa** *("as for")*. Notice that the particle の **no** is needed after the second item and before the preposition. The sentence finishes with です **desu** *(is)*. We are literally saying: *"book as for table on top of is"*.

Practise saying where things are on your CD.

TRACK NUMBER
21

TOPIC 4: Where is it?

Which word?

Put a circle around the alternative
that correctly describes each
picture, as in the example.

1 車は家の （前） です。
　　　　　　　後ろ

2 テレビは窓の 上 です。
　　　　　　　下

3 絵はソファーの 前 です。
　　　　　　　　上

4 コンピュータはテーブルの 上 です。
　　　　　　　　　　　　　となり

5 冷蔵庫はレンジの となり です。
　　　　　　　　　上

6 犬は椅子の 後ろ です。
　　　　　　　下

7 犬は車の 中 です。
　　　　　　下

Language Focus

... があります **... ga arimasu** or ... がいます **... ga imasu** are useful when we wish to express simple descriptive phrases, the equivalent of the English *there is/there are*.

... があります **... ga arimasu** is used when we are talking about *animate* items (e.g., people or animals). がいます **... ga imasu** is used to talk about *inanimate* items (e.g., objects such as books):

本があります。 **hon ga arimasu.**
There is a book./There are some books.

犬がいます。 **inu ga imasu.**
There is a dog./There are some dogs.

To form the question *is there/are there?* simply add か **ka?** on the end:

本がありますか。 **hon ga arimasu ka?**
Is there a book?/Are there any books?

We can now combine this model with the prepositions we have already met to produce fuller descriptions. Notice the word order and the additional particle に **ni** before the second half of the sentence:

テーブルの上に本があります。
teeburu no ue ni hon ga arimasu.
There is a book on the table. (table on top of – book there is)

木の前に犬がいます。 **ki no mae ni inu ga imasu.**
There is a dog in front of the tree. (tree in front of – dog there is)

Look around the room you are in at the moment, or think of a room you know well. Can you describe where some of the things are, using があります **ga arimasu** *or* がいます **ga imasu**?

Where are the mice?

See how many mice you can find in the picture and make sentences about them using the sentence table, as in the example.

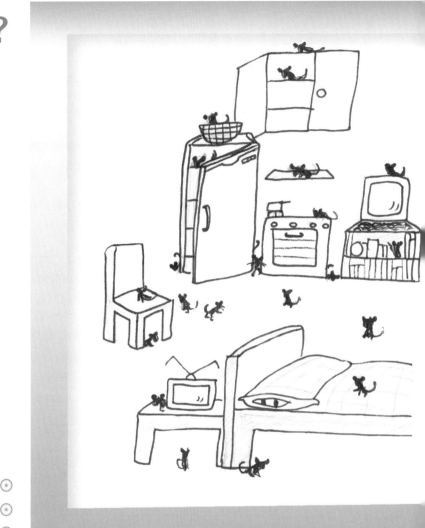

Example:

レンジの前にネズミがいます。

renji no mae ni nezumi ga imasu.

There's a mouse in front of the stove.

テーブル **teeburu**			
椅子 **isu**		中 **naka**	
冷蔵庫 **reizouko**		上 **ue**	
ソファー **sofaa**		下 **shita**	にネズミがいます。
戸棚 **todana**	の **no**		**ni nezumi ga imasu.**
レンジ **renji**		後ろ **ushiro**	
テレビ **terebi**		前 **mae**	
コンピュータ **konpyuuta**		となり **tonari**	
ベッド **beddo**			

Language Focus

We have been using the word です **desu**, meaning *is/am/are,* in many of the sentences we have learnt so far:

日本人です。 **nihonjin desu.** *I'm Japanese.*

セーラさんはイギリス人です。 **seera san wa igirisujin desu.** *Sarah is English.*

本はテレビの上です。 **hon wa terebi no ue desu.** *The book is on top of the television.*

But what if we wish to say that something *is* <u>not</u>? To turn a positive です **desu** statement into a negative one simply change です **desu** to ではありません **de wa arimasen** or じゃありません **ja arimasen**:

日本人ではありません/じゃありません。
nihonjin de wa arimasen/ja arimasen.
I'm not Japanese.

本はテレビの上ではありません/じゃありません。
hon wa terebi no ue de wa arimasen/ja arimasen.
The book is not on top of the television.

To make a があります **ga arimasu**/ がいます **ga imasu** sentence negative change が **ga** to は **wa** and ます **masu** to ません **masen**:

テーブルの上に雑誌はありません。
teeburu no ue ni zasshi wa arimasen.
There isn't a magazine on the table.

ソファーの後ろにネズミはいません。
sofaa no ushiro ni nezumi wa imasen.
There isn't a mouse behind the sofa.

TOPIC 4: Where is it?

No, it isn't!

Practise disagreeing! Go to your audio CD and contradict all the statements you hear.

True or False?

Decide if the sentences describing the picture are true or false, as in the example.

	True	False
部屋には冷蔵庫があります。	☑	☐
部屋にはベッドがあります。	☐	☐
電話はテーブルの上です。	☐	☐
戸棚が二つあります。	☐	☐
窓が二つあります。	☐	☐
テーブルの下に鼠はいません。	☐	☐
家の後ろに木があります。	☐	☐
レンジは冷蔵庫のとなりです。	☐	☐
テーブルの下に犬がいます。	☐	☐
部屋にはテレビはありません。	☐	☐

TOPIC 4: Where is it?

Language Review

You're half way through *Read and Speak Japanese* – congratulations! This is a good time to summarize the main language points covered so far.

1 There are no plural differences in Japanese: 木 **ki** means both *tree* and *trees*.

2 です **desu** (at the end of the sentence) is used to express *am/is/are*. The opposite is ではありません **de wa arimasen** or じゃありません **ja arimasen**.

> 本です。/本ではありません。
> **hon desu. / hon de wa arimasen.** *It's a book./It isn't a book.*

3 You can ask for something by using the phrase … をお願いします … **o onegaishimasu** *(I'd like a/some …)*.

4 は **wa** is used to mark the topic of the sentence and be translated as *"as for"*. か **ka** is the equivalent of the English question mark.

> 安紀子さんは日本人ですか。 **akiko san wa nihon jin desu ka?**
> *Is Akiko Japanese? ("as for Akiko, she is Japanese* **ka***?")*

5 Different words are used for *this/that* depending on the location of the object being talked about: これ **kore** *(object near speaker)*; それ **sore** *(object near listener)*; and あれ **are** *(object far away from speaker and listener)*.

6 Prepositions *(in/on/under, etc.)* in Japanese are placed in different positions in the sentence than in English. *There is/there are* is があります **ga arimasu** for inanimate objects and がいます **ga imasu** for animate beings. The opposites are はありません **wa arimasen** and はいません **wa imasen**. Notice these Japanese structures in comparison with the English:

> 電話は椅子の上です。 **denwa wa isu no ue desu.**
> *The telephone is on the chair.*
>
> ケーキはありません。 **keeki wa arimasen.** *There isn't any cake.*
>
> テーブルの下に犬がいます。 **teeburu no shita ni inu ga imasu.** *There's a dog under the table.*

TOPIC 4: Where is it?

My room

(1) Tear out Game Card 4 at the back of your book and cut out the the small pictures of items around the house (leave the sentence-build cards at the bottom of the sheet for the moment).

(2) Stick the pictures wherever you like on the scene below.

(3) Cut out the sentence-build cards from Game Card 4. Make and say aloud as many sentences as you can describing your room. For example:

| 窓 | の | となり | に | 絵 | があります | 。 |

mado no tonari ni e ga arimasu.

Key Words

大きい	**ookii**	*big*	長い	**nagai**	*long*	
小さい	**chiisai**	*small*	短い	**mijikai**	*short*	
古い	**furui**	*old*	高い	**takai**	*expensive*	
新しい	**atarashii**	*new*	安い	**yasui**	*inexpensive*	
とても	**totemo**	*very*				

TRACK NUMBER
23

Language Focus

⊙ ⊙ ⊙ ⊙ ⊙ Adjectives in Japanese are very easy to use. As in English they can come either before the noun they describe:

> 大きい犬 **ookii inu** *(a) big dog*
>
> 高い車 **takai kuruma** *(an) expensive car*

⊙ ⊙ ⊙ ⊙ Or, in a sentence with **desu** *(am/is/are)*, after the noun they describe. Notice the word order: *item* + **wa** *("as for")* + *adjective* + **desu** *(is)*:

> 犬は大きいです。 **inu wa ookii desu.** *The dog is big.*
>
> 車は高いです。 **kuruma wa takai desu.** *The car is expensive.*

⊙ ⊙ ⊙ とても **totemo** *(very)* is placed in front of the adjective, just like in English:

> とても大きい犬 **totemo ookii inu** *(a) very big dog*
>
> 犬はとても大きいです。 **inu wa totemo ookii desu.**
> *The dog is very big.*

TOPIC 5: What's it like?

Can you remember?

Cover the Key Words panel on page 44. Then see if you can write out the pronunciation and meaning of the words below, as in the example.

安い　　　y _a_ _s_ _u_ i　　　　　_inexpensive_

古い　　　f _ _ _ i　　　　　_____

とても　　t _ _ _ m _　　　　_____

短い　　　_ i _ _ _ a _　　　　_____

小さい　　_ h _ _ s _ _　　　　_____

長い　　　n _ _ _ _ _　　　　_____

大きい　　_ _ _ _ i　　　　_____

新しい　　a _ a _ _ s _ _ _　　　　_____

高い　　　t _ _ _ i　　　　_____

All the adjectives above are written in a combination of kanji characters and a hiragana ending. This is reasonably common in Japanese, and you will meet more examples as you progress.

What does it mean?

Match the Japanese with the pictures. Then read the Japanese out loud and write the English next to each, as in the example.

新しいソファー _____

小さいコーヒー _____

小さい犬 *(a) small dog* _____

とても古い車 _____

小さいネズミ _____

大きいサンドイッチ _____

安い絵 _____

大きい木 _____

Listen and check

Listen to the conversation at the car rental company and decide if these sentences are true or false.

	True	False
1 The conversation takes place in the evening.	☐	☐
2 The woman wants to rent a car.	☐	☐
3 She thinks the first car is too expensive.	☐	☐
4 She thinks the second car is too big.	☐	☐
5 She likes the third car.	☐	☐

Unscramble the sentences

Look at the scrambled sentences below and write the correct order.

Example ("Good morning"):

1

2 ちょっと は です 高い 車

3

4 は ですか どう これ

Language Focus

⊙ ⊙ ⊙ ⊙ ⊙ English uses the verb *to have* when talking about i) personal possession (*I have a car*) and ii) availability of items (*Do you have any sandwiches?* i.e. *Are there any sandwiches?*). Japanese makes a distinction between these two uses.

⊙ ⊙ ⊙ ⊙ When you use the English *have* to mean *possess* the Japanese equivalent is を持っています **o motteimasu**:

> 私は古いコンピュータを持っています。
> **watashi wa furui konpyuuta o motteimasu.**
> *I have an old computer.*

⊙ ⊙ ⊙ To say what someone else owns, use the person's name followed by さん

> ピーターさんは新しい車を持っています。
> **piiitaa san wa atarashii kuruma o motteimasu.**
> *Peter has a new car.*

⊙ ⊙ ⊙ To ask someone if they own a particular item say:
> *name* さん、*item* を持っていますか。

> ヘレンさん、車を持っていますか。
> **heren san, kuruma o motteimasu ka.**
> *Helen, do you have a car?*

⊙ ⊙ When using *have* to express availability, Japanese uses the verbs あります **arimasu** and います **imasu** – which we have met for talking about existence (see page 38). This is useful when enquiring about the availability of goods.

⊙ *Now you can take part in a conversation with the car rental*
⊙ *company. Follow the prompts on your audio CD.*

⊙ *You will need one new phrase:* ちょうどいいですね。
⊙ **choudo ii desu ne.** (That's perfect.)

TOPIC 5: What's it like?

Key Words

足 **ashi**	leg		髪の毛 **kami no ke***	hair	
腕 **ude**	arm		頭 **atama**	head	
指 **yubi**	fingers		鼻 **hana**	nose	
目 **me**	eyes		口 **kuchi**	mouth	
耳 **mimi**	ears		お腹 **onaka**	stomach	

*髪の毛 **kami no ke** is used to refer to human hair (on the head). 毛 **ke** alone means any hair, including animal hair.

By now you're probably feeling much more confident about reading and speaking Japanese. Maybe you'd like to try writing the letters and characters for yourself. Although it's fun to copy the simpler shapes, you will need to get a guide to writing Japanese in order to form them correctly. The strokes should be completed in a certain order and the kanji particularly will need plenty of practice to perfect.

TOPIC 5: What's it like?

Which word?

Circle the correct word to match the translation,
as in the example.

1	*head*	家	頭	椅子	本
2	*leg*	目	窓	鼻	足
3	*stomach*	車	日本	お腹	髪の毛
4	*mouth*	鼻	雑誌	口	猫
5	*fingers*	指	足	目	かばん
6	*hair*	木	足	国	髪の毛
7	*ears*	頭	ドア	市	耳
8	*nose*	指	鼻	ペン	市
9	*eyes*	鼻	電話	目	中国
10	*arm*	腕	犬	頭	指

TOPIC 5: What's it like?

At the pet show

Can you use the words in the box to complete the description of these pets?

1 鼻	**2** です	**3** 耳
4 は	**5** 大きい	**6** 長い

この猫は毛がとても ＿6＿ です。 ＿＿ も長いです。足が小さい＿＿。

この犬 ＿＿ 毛が短いです。 ＿＿ がとても長いです。目が ＿＿ です。

What does it look like?

What does the alien look like? Make as many sentences as you can describing what this creature looks like.

We've included a checklist of features you could describe and adjectives you could use.

Example

髪の毛がとても長いです。

kami no ke ga totemo nagai desu.

He has very long hair.

大きい **ookii** *big*
小さい **chiisai** *small*
長い **nagai** *long*
短い **mijikai** *short*
とても **totemo** *very*

足 **ashi** *leg*
腕 **ude** *arm*
指 **yubi** *fingers*
目 **me** *eyes*
耳 **mimi** *ears*
髪の毛 **kami no ke** *hair*
頭 **atama** *head*
鼻 **hana** *nose*
口 **kuchi** *mouth*
お腹 **onaka** *stomach*

TOPIC 5: What's it like?

What do you have?

1. Cut out set 1 picture cards from Game Card 5 and put them in a bag.

2. Cut out set 2 adjective cards and put them in a different bag.

3. Pull out one card from each bag without looking.

4. Make a sentence to match the cards you have chosen, for example:

   私は古いコンピュータを持っています。
   watashi wa furui konpyuuta o motteimasu.
   (*I have an old computer.*)

5. Keep playing until all the cards have been chosen.

6. You can put the cards back in the bag and start again – each time the sentences will be different.

Key Words

27

空港 **kuukou**	*airport*	公園 **kouen**	*park*
学校 **gakkou**	*school*	橋 **hashi**	*bridge*
ホテル **hoteru**	*hotel*	道 **michi**	*street*
銀行 **ginkou**	*bank*	なかみせ通り **nakamise doori**	*Nakamise St.*
レストラン **resutoran**	*restaurant*	...はどこですか。 **... wa doko desu ka?**	*where is/are...?*
駅 **eki**	*station*	あそこ **asoko**	*over there*

28

You are new in town and are asking a Japanese friend about the facilities. Follow the prompts on your audio CD.

TOPIC 6: How do I get there?

Language Focus

○ ○ ○ ○ ○ Notice the words for *hotel* and *restaurant*. They are examples of 外来語 **gairaigo** words borrowed from other languages. Japanese has borrowed many words from other languages, particularly English. Look back at Topic 3. The words for *sandwich*, *cake*, and *coffee* are all examples of **gairaigo**.

○ ○ ○ ○ You can recognize these words although they will sound slightly different and often longer since they are adapted to Japanese pronunciation. **Gairaigo** words are always written in katakana script.

Questions and answers

Match the questions with their answers, as in the example.

銀行はどこですか。   橋はあそこです。

レストランはありますか。   はい、レストランがあります。

ホテルはありますか。   公園は学校のとなりです。

公園はどこですか。   銀行は学校のとなりです。

橋はどこですか。   駅の前にホテルがあります。

Key Words

TRACK NUMBER
29

タクシー **takushii**	*taxi*	
バス **basu**	*bus*	
電車 **densha**	*train*	

船 **fune**	*boat*	
自転車 **jitensha**	*bicycle*	
飛行機 **hikouki**	*plane*	

Language Focus

⊙ ⊙ ⊙ ⊙ ⊙ The particle で **de** can be used after a mode of transportation to mean *by*.

車で **kuruma de** *by car*

タクシーで **takushii de** *by taxi*

バスで **basu de** *by bus*

船で **fune de** *by boat*

TOPIC 6: How do I get there?

Word Square

Can you find the 7 different means of transportation in the word square?
Write out the meaning for the words you have found, as in the example.

駅	船	ラ	ソ	飛	行	機	ル
か	ば	ん	ス	レ	髪	港	ン
バ	公	で	さ	ビ	園	電	車
ー	タ	ク	シ	ー	フ	ク	す
こ	コ	ン	ピ	ュ	ー	タ	あ
レ	ー	毛	い	腹	テ	ら	そ
ト	バ	ス	う	の	な	車	こ
道	フ	ァ	自	転	車	子	シ

kuruma *(car)*

_____

_____

_____

_____

_____

_____

Key Words

TRACK NUMBER
30

すみません。 *excuse me!*
sumimasen

まっすぐ行って下さい
massugu itte kudasai
go straight ahead

... はどうやって行きますか。
... wa dou yatte ikimasu ka?
How do I get to ...?

電車で行きます
densha de ikimasu *go by train*

曲がる **magaru** *to turn*

タクシーで行きます
takushii de ikimasu *go by taxi*

... 曲がって下さい *please turn ...*
... magatte kudasai

それから **sore kara** *then*

右 **migi** *right*

博物館 **hakubutsukan** *museum*

左 **hidari** *left*

バス停 **basutei** *bus stop*

TRACK NUMBER
31

⊙
⊙ *Ask for directions to places around town.*
⊙ *Follow the prompts on your audio CD.*
⊙

TOPIC 6: How do I get there?

Language Focus

To ask for directions use ... はどこですか。 ... **wa doko desu ka?** *(Where is/are ...?)* or ... はどうやって行きますか。 ... **wa dou yatte ikimasu ka?** *(How do I get to ...?)*:

銀行はどこですか。 **ginkou wa doko desu ka?**

Where is the bank?

公園はどうやって行きますか。 **kouen wa dou yatte ikimasu ka?** *How do I get to the park?*

When replying, the direction 右 **migi** *(right)* or 左 **hidari** *(left)* comes first in the sentence, followed by the particle **ni** and then 曲がって下さい **magatte kudasai** *(please turn)*:

右に曲がって下さい。　　左に曲がって下さい。

migi ni magatte kudasai.　**hidari ni magatte kudasai.**

(Please) turn right.　　*(Please) turn left.*

Here are two possible dialogues:

– すみません、駅はどこですか。

　sumimasen, eki wa doko desu ka? *Excuse me. Where's the station?*

– まっすぐ行って下さい。それから右に曲がって下さい。駅はホテルのとなりです。 **massugu itte kudasai.**
　sore kara migi ni magatte kudasai. eki wa hoteru no tonari desu.

　Go straight ahead. Then turn right. The station is next to the hotel.

– すみません、空港はどうやって行きますか。
　sumimasen, kuukou wa dou yatte ikimasu ka?

　Excuse me. How do I get to the airport?

– バスで行きます。 **basu de ikimasu.** *Go by bus.*

TOPIC 6: How do I get there?

Which way?

Make questions and answers, as in the example.

すみません、駅はどこですか。
sumimasen, eki wa doko desu ka?
Excuse me, where's the station?

左に曲がって下さい。
hidari ni magatte kudasai.
Turn left.

1

2

3

4

5

6

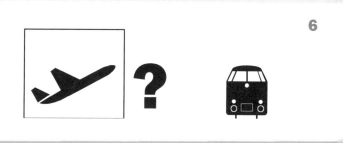

TOPIC 6: How do I get there?

Around town

Below is a plan of a small town with some landmarks shown.
Starting from *You are here*, try to give directions to the following places:

駅	ホテル	公園	バス停
eki	**hoteru**	**kouen**	**basutei**
the station	*the hotel*	*the park*	*the bus stop*

For example, your directions to the station could be something like this:

まっすぐ行って下さい。それから右に曲がって下さい。駅は橋のとなりです。
massugu itte kudasai. sore kara migi ni magatte kudasai. eki wa hashi no tonari desu.
Go straight ahead. Then turn right. The station is next to the bridge.

Unscramble the conversation

See if you can read the Japanese in the word balloons. Then put the conversation into the correct order.

バス停はどこですか。 **a**

左に曲がって下さい。
バス停は銀行のとなりです。 **b**

なかみせ通りですか。
バスで行きます。 **c**

すみませんが, なかみせ通り **e**
はどこですか。

ありがとうございます。**d**

ORDER: _e,_ _____

Check your answer with the conversation on your audio CD.

TRACK NUMBER
32

TOPIC 6: How do I get there?

Town Planning

TRACK NUMBER **33**

1. Cut out the pictures of places around town from Game Card 6.

2. Listen to the first set of directions for the bank on your audio CD.

3. Pause the CD and stick the picture of the bank in the correct place on the town map on your game card.

4. Listen to the next set of directions and stick down the appropriate picture.

5. Repeat for all the directions until you have all your pictures stuck down on the map.

6. Looking at the completed map, you could try to give directions to the various places yourself. For example:

まっすぐ行って下さい。
それから左に曲がって下さい。
銀行は学校のとなりです。

maassugu itte kudasai. sore kara hidari ni magatte kudasai. ginkou wa gakkou no tonari desu.

(*Go straight ahead. Then turn left. The bank is next to the school.*)

Key Words

妻	**tsuma**	*my wife*	奥さん	**okusan**	*wife*
夫	**otto**	*my husband*	ご主人	**goshujin**	*husband*
母	**haha**	*my mother*	お母さん	**okaasan**	*mother*
父	**chichi**	*my father*	お父さん	**otousan**	*father*
姉	**ane**	*my older sister*	お姉さん	**oneesan**	*older sister*
妹	**imouto**	*my younger sister*	妹さん	**imoutosan**	*younger sister*
兄	**ani**	*my older brother*	お兄さん	**oniisan**	*older brother*
弟	**otouto**	*my younger brother*	弟さん	**otoutosan**	*younger brother*
娘	**musume**	*my daughter*	お嬢さん	**ojousan**	*daughter*
息子	**musuko**	*my son*	息子さん	**musukosan**	*son*
			子供	**kodomo**	*children*

Japanese has two sets of words for family members, one meaning <u>my</u> mother, <u>my</u> older sister, etc., and one meaning someone else's mother, older sister, etc. The meaning of my, your, *etc. is communicated within the word itself and there is no need for a separate word to express possession.*

TOPIC 7: Who's this?

Language Focus

You can make sentences to talk about your family using the verb がいます **ga imasu** *(to exist: for living objects)* and its opposite はいません **wa imasen**, which you have already met (see pages 38 and 40):

> 姉がいます。 **ane ga imasu.**
> *I have an (older) sister. ("An older sister exists.")*
>
> 娘がいます。 **musume ga imasu.**
> *I have a daughter.*
>
> 弟はいません。 **otouto wa imasen.**
> *I don't have a younger brother.*

What does it mean?

Join the English to the pronunciation and the Japanese script, as in the example.

children	**oniisan**	お父さん
my husband	**otouto**	奥さん
older brother	**kodomo**	お姉さん
my daughter	**chichi**	息子さん
father	**goshujin**	ご主人
my mother	**musukosan**	お兄さん
older sister	**imoutosan**	妹さん
my younger brother	**otousan**	子供
wife	**otto**	父
husband	**musume**	弟
younger sister	**haha**	娘
son	**okusan**	母
my father	**oneesan**	夫

TOPIC 7: Who's this?

Language Focus

⊙ ⊙ ⊙ ⊙ ⊙ You have seen that when talking about your own family the concept of *my* is communicated within the word itself and there is no need for a separate word to express possession. Similarly, when addressing someone else about their family you would not need a separate word for *your*:

> ロバートさん、弟さんがいますか。 **robaato san, otoutosan ga imasu ka?** *Robert, do you have a younger brother?*
>
> はい、弟がいます。 **hai, otouto ga imasu.**
> *Yes, I have a younger brother.*
>
> 弟さんの名前は何ですか。 **otoutosan no namae wa nan desu ka?** *What's your younger brother's name?*
>
> 弟の名前はピーターです。 **otouto no namae wa piitaa desu.** *My younger brother's name is Peter.*

⊙ ⊙ ⊙ Now look again at the last two sentences. Here we can see examples of how other possessives are formed in Japanese. The particle の **no** between 弟さん **otoutosan** and 名前 **namae** is the equivalent of the English *'s* as in *Jane's pen* and is used to express possession.

When の **no** is used together with the word for *I*, the meaning becomes *my*:

> 私のペン **watashi no pen** *my pen*
>
> 私の車は小さいです。
> **watashi no kuruma wa chiisai desu.** *My car is small.*

⊙ ⊙ Remember that when expressing *your*, *his*, *her*, etc., Japanese prefers to use people's names rather than pronouns.

> 亜紀子さんの猫は大きいです。 **akikosan no neko wa ookii desu.** *Her (Akiko's) cat is big.*
>
> 優子さんのコンピュータは小さいですね。
> **yuuko san no konpyuuta wa chiisai desu ne.**
> *Yuuko, your computer is small, isn't it?*

TOPIC 7: Who's this?

If we wish to use a possessive to say that something or someone belongs to something or someone else then we would combine の **no** with the structure we learned earlier ...は ...です。 **... wa ... desu.**

> ピーターさんはロバートさんのお兄さんです。
> **piitaa san wa robaato san no oniisan desu.**
> *Peter is Robert's older brother.*

Family Tree

Make up sentences about this family, as in the example.
Don't forget to use the words for talking about someone else's family

優子さんは実さんの妹さんです。

yuuko san wa minoru san no imoutosan desu.

Yuuko is Minoru's younger sister.

Robert's family

Listen to Robert answering questions about his family.
Circle the correct names on the family tree, as in the example.

ピーター
ケン
マーク

セーラ
ヘレン
メリー

ロバート
ケン
ロバート

ロバート
マーク
ピーター

Questions and answers

Now read the questions on the left and then match them to the answers on the right that Robert gave, as in the example.

お名前は？

ご兄弟がいますか。

お母さんの名前は何ですか。

お兄さんの名前は何ですか。

お父さんの名前は何ですか。

どこから来ましたか。

ロンドンから来ました。

父の名前はケンです。

兄がいます。

ロバートです。

母の名前はヘレンです。

兄の名前はピーターです。

TOPIC 7: Who's this?

Language Focus

A useful phrase for introducing people is:

> こちらは … さんです。 **kochira wa … san desu.**
> *This is …*

However, if you are introducing a member of your own family you do not need to say こちらは **kochira wa**. You can also omit さん **san** after the name:

> 妹のセーラです。 **imouto no Seera desu.**
> *This is my younger sister Sarah.*

Don't forget to add さん **san** after the person's name if they are not a member of your own family, as a sign of respect.

> – セーラさん, こんにちは。 **seera san konnichiwa.**
> *Hello, Sarah.*
>
> – メリーさん, こんにちは。 **merii san konnichiwa.**
> *Hello, Mary.*
>
> – 兄のマークです。 **ani no maaku desu.**
> *This is my (older) brother, Mark.*
>
> – はじめまして、マークさん。セーラです。
> **hajimemashite, maaku san. seera desu.**
> *Pleased to meet you, Mark. I'm Sarah.*
>
> – はじめまして、セーラさん。 **hajimemashite, seera san.** *Pleased to meet you, Sarah.*

Now introduce your family. Follow the prompts on your audio CD.

Key Words

一	**ichi**	*one*	六	**roku**	*six*
二	**ni**	*two*	七	**nana/shichi**	*seven*
三	**san**	*three*	八	**hachi**	*eight*
四	**shi/yon**	*four*	九	**kyu/ku**	*nine*
五	**go**	*five*	十	**juu**	*ten*

Language Focus

⊙ ⊙ ⊙ ⊙ ⊙ The numbers listed above are those which would be used for counting on your fingers and for doing arithmetic. To make higher numbers we simply combine the numbers 1 to 10. For example 11 (10 + 1) = 十一 **juuichi**, 20 (2 x 10) = 二十 **nijuu**, 52 (5 x 10 + 2) = 五十二 **gojuuni**. The second pronunciation for 4 and 7 above is used in combinations, e.g. 40 = 四十 **yonjuu** *not* **shijuu**.

⊙ ⊙ ⊙ ⊙ ⊙ To count objects in Japanese is more complicated. We cannot use this set of numbers. Every object has a *classifier*, which is used for this purpose. The classifier is put after the number, often completely altering the pronunciation.

⊙ ⊙ ⊙ For example, the classifier for counting people (including family members) is 人 **nin** which we met when talking about nationality:

一人	**hitori**	*1 person*	六人	**rokunin**	*6 people*
二人	**futari**	*2 people*	七人	**shichinin**	*7 people*
三人	**sannin**	*3 people*	八人	**hachinin**	*8 people*
四人	**yonin**	*4 people*	九人	**kyuunin**	*9 people*
五人	**gonin**	*5 people*	十人	**juunin**	*10 people*

TOPIC 7: Who's this?

How many?

Match the numbers to the pronunciation, as in the example.

四　　　　　　　　　　　**hachi**

五　　　　　　　　　　　**juu**

六　　　　　　　　　　　**go**

十　　　　　　　　　　　**roku**

一　　　　　　　　　　　**kyu/ku**

九　　　　　　　　　　　**san**

八　　　　　　　　　　　**shi/yon**

二　　　　　　　　　　　**ichi**

七　　　　　　　　　　　**ni**

三　　　　　　　　　　　**nana/shichi**

Japanese sums

Circle the correct answer to these sums, as in the example.

1　一 + 三 =　　一、二、三、④、五、六、七、八、九、十

2　四 + 二 =　　一、二、三、四、五、六、七、八、九、十

3　二 x 三 =　　一、二、三、四、五、六、七、八、九、十

4　五 + 三 =　　一、二、三、四、五、六、七、八、九、十

5　六 – 二 =　　一、二、三、四、五、六、七、八、九、十

6　七 + 三 =　　一、二、三、四、五、六、七、八、九、十

7　九 – 四 =　　一、二、三、四、五、六、七、八、九、十

8　八 + 一 =　　一、二、三、四、五、六、七、八、九、十

9　　　　　　　　　　　　　　　　　　　　　　　　　　　

10　六 – 五 =　　一、二、三、四、五、六、七、八、九、十

My family

Use the table below to make sentences about yourself, as in the examples.

姉が二人います。 **ane ga futari imasu.** *I have two (older) sisters.*

子供はいません。 **kodomo wa imasen.** *I don't have any children.*

姉 **ane**		一人 **hitori**	
妹 **imouto**	兄 **ga**	二人 **futari**	います。 **imasu.**
兄 **ani**		三人 **sannin**	
弟 **otouto**			
息子 **musuko**			
娘 **musume**	は **wa**	いません。 **imasen.**	
子供 **kodomo**			

Listen and speak

TRACK NUMBER
38

Now imagine you are with some of your family looking for the station and you meet a Japanese friend.

Prepare carefully the information below you will need to take part in the conversation. Then go to your audio CD and see how you get on introducing your family.

1 Think of two members of your family – one male and one female. For example, your husband and your daughter; or your brother and your mother.

2 How would you tell someone their names in Japanese?

3 How would you ask *How do I get to the station?*

4 How do you say *thank you* and *goodbye*?

You can repeat the conversation, but this time use two different members of your family and ask how to get to the bus stop.

TOPIC 7: Who's this?

Bingo!

1. Cut out the small number tokens and the bingo cards on Game Card 7.

2. Find 16 buttons for each player or make 16 small blank pieces of card (to cover the squares on the bingo card).

3. Put the tokens into a bag and shake thoroughly.

4. Pull out a number token and say the number out loud in Japanese.

5. If you have that number on your card, cover the square with a button or blank piece of card. If you have more than one square with that number, you can only cover one.

6. Put the number token back in the bag and shake again.

7. Repeat steps 3–6 until you have all the squares covered on the bingo card. Then you can shout: ヤッタ **yatta!** (*I've won!*)

   You can play with a friend or challenge yourself.

Key Words

TRACK NUMBER
39

先生 **sensei** *teacher*

学生 **gakusei** *student*

医者 **isha** *doctor*

サラリーマン

sarariiman *office worker*

店員 **ten'in** *store assistant*

運転手 **untenshu** *driver*

コック **kokku** *cook/chef*

俳優 **haiyuu** *actor*

技師 **gishi** *engineer*

会計士 **kaikeishi** *accountant*

If your job or those of your family aren't listed here, try to find out what they are in Japanese.

TOPIC 8: What do you do?

What does it mean?

Join the Japanese to the pronunciation and the English, as in the example.

学生	kaikeishi	office worker
会計士	sarariiman	accountant
運転手	ten'in	actor
サラリーマン	gishi	driver
俳優	gakusei	store assistant
店員	isha	engineer
先生	kokku	doctor
医者	untenshu	cook/chef
コック	sensei	teacher
技師	haiyuu	student

The tools of the trade

Match the jobs to the tools of the trade, as in the example.

Language Focus

⊙ ⊙ ⊙ ⊙ ⊙ To ask someone what they do for a living, use the following question:

お仕事は何ですか。
oshigoto wa nan desu ka.
What's your job? ("As for job, what is it?")

⊙ ⊙ ⊙ ⊙ The answer is simple – just give the job followed byです **desu.**

医者です。 **isha desu.** *I'm a doctor.*

先生です。 **sensei desu.** *I'm a teacher.*

⊙ ⊙ ⊙ Other possible answers include:

退職しました。
taishoku shimashita.
I'm retired.

働いていません。
hataraiteimasen.
I'm not working at the moment.

TOPIC 8: What do you do?

Listen and note

TRACK NUMBER
40

Listen to two people telling you about themselves
and fill out the details in English on the forms below.

First name: ..... *Akiko* .....

Family name: .....

Nationality: .....

Name of spouse: .....

No. of children: .....

Occupation: .....

First name: .....

Family name: .....

Nationality: .....

Name of spouse: .....

No. of children: .....

Occupation: .....

Your turn to speak

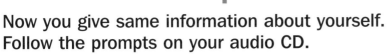

TRACK NUMBER
41

Now you give same information about yourself.
Follow the prompts on your audio CD.

What's the answer?

Match the questions to the answers.
For example: 1d

1 お名前は何ですか。

2 どこから来ましたか。

a 息子がひとりと娘が二人います。

b 俳優です。

3 奥さんの名前は何ですか。

オーストラリアから来ました。
c

4 お子さんがいますか。

d ハリーです。

5 お仕事は何ですか。

e 妻の名前はジュリーです。

Which word?

Write the correct number of the word in the box to complete the description, as in the example.

| 1 子供 2 娘 3 俳優 |
| 4 妻 5 一人 |
| 6 です 7 オーストラリア |

ハリーです。___3___ です。

_____ のメルボーンから来ました。

_____ の名前はジュリー_____。

_____ が三人います。息子が____

と____ が二人います。

Key Words

工場 **koujou**	factory	
病院 **byouin**	hospital	
店 **mise**	store	
劇場 **gekijou**	theatre	

事務所 **jimusho**   office

大学 **daigaku**   college/ university

Look back as well at the Key Words on page 54 for other places of work.

TRACK NUMBER 42

Language Focus

⊙ ⊙ ⊙ ⊙ ⊙ 勤めています **tsutometeimasu** *(to work)* can be used together with the particle に **ni** to say *where* you work. The work-place comes first in the sentence:

医者です。病院に勤めています。
isha desu. byouin ni tsutometeimasu.
I'm a doctor. I work in a hospital.

⊙ ⊙ ⊙ ⊙ We can be more specific about where we work by adding a town or city. Notice the use of the particle の **no** to link the town/city and the place of work:

医者です。大阪の病院に勤めています。
isha desu. oosaka no byouin ni tsutometeimasu.
I am a doctor. I work in a hospital in Osaka.

⊙ ⊙ ⊙ To ask where someone works you would say:

どこに勤めていますか。
doko ni tsutometeimasu ka.
Where do you work?

TOPIC 8: What do you do?

Word Square

Can you find the 8 different work-places in the word square?
Words can read horizontally or vertically.

Write out the meaning for the words you have found.

事	工	場	ソ	テ	ー	ブ	ル
か	ば	ん	ス	病	髪	場	ン
さ	公	で	さ	院	園	車	場
お	店	空	劇	場	レ	銀	行
こ	大	学	ピ	ュ	ス	タ	あ
レ	ー	毛	い	腹	ト	事	そ
ト	院	誌	う	の	ラ	務	こ
ソ	フ	ァ	ー	場	ン	所	シ

factory

_____

_____

_____

_____

_____

_____

_____

Now make sentences for each of the work-places, as in the example:

技師です。 工場に 勤めています。

gishi desu. koujou ni tsutometeimasu.

I'm an engineer. I work in a factory.

What are they saying?

Match the people with what they are saying. For example: 1e

1 東京のレストランに勤めています。

4 大阪の店に勤めています。

2 イギリスの学校に勤めています。

5 俳優です。

3 アメリカの銀行に勤めています。

6 カナダの工場に勤めています。

a

b

c

d

e

f

TOPIC 8: What do you do?

Listen and speak

TRACK NUMBER
43

Imagine you are a chef. You're meeting someone
for the first time and they are asking you about yourself.

Prepare carefully the information below you will need to take part in the conversation. Then go to your audio CD and see how you get on talking about yourself.

1 Your name is Minoru (実).

2 You're from Tokyo.

3 You're a chef.

4 You work in a Japanese restaurant in New York.

5 You have two daughters.

6 Your wife is a teacher in a big school.

Which word?

Now write the correct number of the word in the box to complete
the description of Minoru's life, as in the example.

1 勤めています	2 四人	3 から	4 娘
5 学生	6 先生	7 レストラン	8 学校

はじめまして。実です。東京 __3__ 来ました。コックです。

ニューヨークの _____ に _____ 。家族とニューヨークに住んでいます。

_____ 家族です。妻と _____ が二人います。妻は _____ です。

レストランのとなりに日本の学校があります。この _____ に勤めています。

娘はニューヨーク大学の _____ です。

Where do I work?

1. Tear out the work-place picture cards and profession word cards on Game Card 8.

2. Turn the cards face down on a table, with the pictures on one end of the table and the words on the other.

3. Turn a word card and say …です**… desu** (*I'm a …*) as appropriate, e.g. 先生です **sensei desu** (*I'm a teacher).*

4. Then turn a picture card. If the work-place picture matches the profession, say …に勤めています **… ni tsutometeimasu** (*I work in a/an …),* e.g. 学校に勤めています **gakkou ni tsutometeimasu** (*I work in a school).*

5. If you turn a matching picture and say both sentences correctly, you get to keep the cards. If you don't, you must turn the cards face down and try again.

6. The winner is the one who collects the most cards.

7. You can compete with a friend or challenge yourself against the clock.

(Review the vocabulary on pages 54, 56 and 74 before you play the game.)

This **Test Yourself** section reviews all the Japanese you have learnt in this programme. Have a go at the activities. If you find you have forgotten something, go back to the relevant topic(s) and look again at the **Key Words** and **Language Focus** panels.

May I have...?

Ask for the following, as in the example:

紅茶をお願いします。
koocha o onegaishimasu.

1

2

3

4

5

6

Listen and check

Listen to Akiko talking about herself and decide if the following sentences are true or false.

		True	False
1	Akiko is Japanese.	☐	☐
2	She comes from a small town.	☐	☐
3	She's a teacher.	☐	☐
4	She works in France.	☐	☐
5	Her husband is an engineer.	☐	☐
6	She has five children.	☐	☐

Which word?

Now write the correct number of the word in the box to complete the description of Akiko, as in the example.

1 子供	2 大きい	3 勤めています	4 夫
5 一人	6 来ました	7 先生	8 娘

はじめまして。亜紀子です。大阪から __6__ 。大阪は ____ 市です。

私は ____ です。イギリスにある日本の学校に ____ 。 ____ は医者です。

日本の学校のとなりに大きい病院があります。夫はこの病院に勤めています。

____ が四人います。 ____ が三人と息子が ____ います。

Can you try and make up a similar description about yourself?

Read and check

Look at the picture and decide if the sentences are true or false.
Look back at topics 4–6 if you are unsure of any of the words.

		True	False
1	銀行があります。	❏	❏
2	銀行の右に病院があります。	❏	❏
3	銀行の左に学校があります。	❏	❏
4	犬がいます。	❏	❏
5	車はありません。	❏	❏
6	車の上に小さい猫がいます。	❏	❏
7	学校の後ろに大きい木があります。	❏	❏
8	病院の前に古い自転車があります。	❏	❏

What does it mean?

Can you remember these words? Join the words and write the pronunciation next to the Japanese, as in the example

my children	息子	*musuko*
my husband	父	
my son	母	
my daughter	妹	
my father	兄	
my mother	姉	
my younger sister	子供	
my older brother	夫	
my older sister	娘	
my wife	弟	
my younger brother	妻	

How do you say it?

Now see if you can say these in Japanese, as in the example.

1 My husband is a doctor.
夫は医者です。
otto wa isha desu.

2 I have a younger sister.

3 Our son is an engineer.

4 Minoru is Yuuko's older brother.

5 My wife's name is Sarah.

6 Her younger brother is an actor.

7 I don't have any children.

8 I have three daughters.

TEST YOURSELF

At the tourist information office

TRACK NUMBER

45

Finally, you are going to test your new Japanese conversational skills by joining in the dialogue on your audio CD.

You're going to ask for some information at a tourist information office.

To prepare, first see if you can remember these words and phrases. Write the pronunciation and English next to the Japanese, as in the example.

さようなら	_sayounara_ _goodbye_
博物館	
バス停	
左に曲がって下さい	
おはようございます	
どこ	
後ろ	
ありがとうございます	
上	
駅	

Now follow the prompts on your audio CD. Don't worry if you don't manage everything the first time around. Just keep repeating it until you are fluent.

⊙ ⊙ ⊙ ⊙ ⊙ Congratulations on successfully completing this introductory *Read and Speak Japanese* programme. You have overcome the obstacle of learning a new language in an unfamiliar script. You should now have the confidence to enjoy using the Japanese you have learnt. You have also acquired a sound basis from which to expand your language skills in whichever direction you choose. Good luck!

This **Reference** section gives an overview of the Japanese script and pronunciation. You can use it to refer to as you work your way through the *Read and Speak Japanese* programme. Don't expect to take it all in from the beginning. The programme is designed to build your confidence step by step as you progress through the topics. The details will start to fall into place gradually as you become more familiar with the Japanese characters and language.

The Japanese script

No one can pretend that the Japanese writing system is simple. For historic reasons, the Japanese language is written in a combination of three different writing systems: *kanji*, the Chinese system of ideograms adopted by Japanese; *hiragana*, a script used mainly for words of Japanese origin; and *katakana*, a script used to write foreign loan words, of which there are many.

Although it is possible to write all words in katakana, and indeed this is how Japanese children first learn to write, there is a commonly-accepted way of writing a particular word and this is one you would see in everyday life. This programme presents the words and phrases as they are normally written.

Kanji (Chinese Characters)

Kanji is not an alphabet, but a series of ideograms, or *characters*. These characters originally evolved in China out of pictograms used as a writing system by primitive hunters and were then adopted by Japanese. A few characters still resemble the object or concept they refer to, but most have changed beyond recognition.

Japanese uses kanji to write basic words and concepts. Most words connected with the natural world or universal concepts, such as *big* and *cat*, will be represented by kanji, or a combination of kanji with added hiragana.

Some words consist of a single kanji, others are made up of two or more characters:

家 **ie** *house*	学校 **gakkou** *school*
猫 **neko** *cat*	運転手 **untenshu** *driver*

There is no way of working out the pronunciation of kanji. You will need to learn them on an individual basis.

Katakana and Hiragana

⊙ ⊙ ⊙ ⊙ ⊙ Although often referred to as an *alphabets,* katakana and hiragana are actually *syllabaries.* Each character represents a syllable (a consonant plus a vowel), such as **ha** or **fu.** You will find the katakana and hiragana syllabaries opposite, but do not try to learn them by heart. It is better to give these tables a quick glance and then move on to the topics. As you meet each word or phrase, you can refer to the tables if you want to work out the individual characters.

⊙ ⊙ ⊙ ⊙ The signs ˝ and ° are used to add further sounds to the characters in the tables. In addition, a long dash (ー) is used to lengthen a sound in some katakana words. For example, the katakana character テ **te** is lengthened to テー **tee** by adding this dash:

> テーブル **teeberu** *table*
> セーラ **seera** *Sarah*

⊙ ⊙ ⊙ Hiragana is sometimes used to write complete words:

> こんにちは **konnichiwa** *hello*
> そば **soba** *noodles*

⊙ ⊙ But many others are made up of a kanji ideogram with a hiragana ending:

> 古い **furui** *old*
> 後ろ **ushiro** *behind*

⊙ The structural words and grammatical particles which "glue" the language together tend to be written in hiragana, for example です **desu** *(am/is/are)*, は **wa** *(topic marker "as for")*, and か **ka** *(question marker).* Watching out for these will help you to break up sentences and questions into their component parts:

> お名前は何ですか。 **onamae <u>wa</u> nan <u>desu</u> <u>ka</u>?**
>
> *What is your name? ("name as for what is it")*

Hiragana Syllabary

あ a	か ka	さ sa	た ta	な na	は ha	ま ma	や ya	ら ra	わ wa
い i	き ki	し shi	ち chi	に ni	ひ hi	み mi		れ ri	
う u	く ku	す su	つ tsu	ぬ nu	ふ fu	む mu	ゆ yu	る ru	
え e	け ke	せ se	て te	ね ne	へ he	め me		れ re	
お o	こ ko	そ so	と to	の no	ほ ho	も mo	よ yo	ろ ro	を wo
				ん n					

Katakana Syllabary

ア a	カ ka	サ sa	タ ta	ナ na	ハ ha	マ ma	ヤ ya	ラ ra	ワ wa
イ i	キ ki	シ shi	チ chi	ニ ni	ヒ hi	ミ mi		リ ri	
ウ u	ク ku	ス su	ツ tsu	ヌ nu	フ fu	ム mu	ユ yu	ル ru	
エ e	ケ ke	セ se	テ te	ネ ne	ヘ he	メ me		レ re	
オ o	コ ko	ソ so	ト to	ノ no	ホ ho	モ mo	ヨ yo	ロ ro	ヲ wo
				ン n					

Pronunciation

The syllables in Japanese are pronounced equally and there is no particular emphasis on any part of the word. Many letters are pronounced in a similar way to English, but look out for these more unfamiliar sounds:

f   a Japanese **f** is pronounced without putting your lower teeth over your upper lip

r   somewhere between the English *r* and *l*

w   pronounced with slack rather than rounded lips

You will find an introduction to the sounds of Japanese on track 1 of your audio CD.

Topic 1

Page 6
Check your answers with the Key Words panel on page 5.

Page 8: What are they saying?

Page 8: What do you hear?
You should have ticked boxes 2 and 5.

Page 10: What does it mean?
1b, 2f, 3e, 4a, 5d, 6c

Page 10: Which word?
おはよう __2__.
__5__ ございます。
安紀子__4__。お名前__3__。
__1__ です。

Page 11: What are their names?

セーラ	**seera** *Sarah*	ピーター	**piittaa** *Peter*
ヘレン	**heren** *Helen*	ケン	**ken** *Ken*
メリー	**Merii** *Mary*	マーク	**maaku** *Mark*
リサ	**risa** *Lisa*	ロバート	**robaato** *Robert*
ハナ	**hana** *Hannah*	ジェームス	**jeemusu** *James*

Page 12: In or out?
IN: Sarah, Minoru, Yuuko, Ken, Tadashi
OUT: James, Robert, Akiko, Helen, Mary

Topic 2

Page 15: Where are the countries?
カナダ 1　　イギリス 4　　日本 6　　オーストラリア 8
韓国 7　　アイルランド 3 アメリカ 2　　中国 5

Page 16: How do you say it?
Check your answers with the Key Words panel on page 14.

Page 16: Where are the cities?
東京は日本にあります。 **toukyou wa nihon ni arimasu.**
大阪は日本にあります。 **oosaka wa nihon ni arimasu.**
ニューヨークはアメリカにあります。
nyuuyooku wa amerika ni arimasu.
シドニーはオーストラリアにあります。
shidonii wa oosutoraria ni arimasu.
ワシントンはアメリカにあります。
washinton wa amerika ni arimasu.
ロンドンはイギリスにあります。
rondon wa igirisu ni arimasu.
ロサンジェルスはアメリカにあります。
rosanjerusu wa amerika ni arimasu.
ダブリンはアイルランドにあります。
daburin wa airurando ni arimasu.

Page 17: Audio track 8
Akiko: Japan; Mary: Australia; Sarah: England; Ken: China

Page 18: Where are they from?

Page 20: Who's from where?
1 ピーターさんはアメリカ人です。
　 piitaa san wa amerikajin desu.

2 優子さんは日本人です。 **yuuko san wa nihonjin desu.**

3 リサさんはカナダ人です。 **risa san wa kandajin desu.**

4 マークさんはオーストラリア人です。
　 maaku san wa oosutorariajin desu.

5 ジェームスさんはアイルランド人です。
　 jeemusu san wa airurandojin desu.

6 スンさんは韓国人です。 **sun san wa kankokujin desu.**

7 実さんは日本人です。 **minoru san wa nihonjin desu.**

8 メリーさんはイギリス人です。 **merii san wa igirisujin desu.**

Page 21: Listen and Check

1 False; 2 True; 3 True; 4 True; 5 False

Page 21: What does it mean?

I'm from Canada.	はじめまして。
He's from Japan.	カナダ人です。
My name's Lucy.	お名前は？
What's your name?	日本人です。
How do you do?	どうぞよろしく。
Pleased to meet you.	ルーシーです。

Page 22: What does it mean?

1 ルーシーです。 **My name is Lucy.**

2 カナダ人です。 **I'm Canadian.**

3 優子さんは日本人です。 **Yuuko is Japanese.**

4 お名前は？ **What's your name?**

5 安紀子です。 **I'm Akiko.**

6 ピーターさんは何人ですか。 **What nationality is Peter?** *or* **Peter, what nationality are you?**

7 ジェームスさんはイギリス人です。 **James is English.**

8 アメリカ人です。 **I'm American.**

Topic 3

Page 25

Check your answers with the Key Words panel on page 24.

Page 26: Word Square

computer, sofa, bag, magazine, book, chair, television, table

Page 26: Odd One Out

椅子 ＊ テーブル ＊ （お名前） ＊ ソファー

（電話） 日本 ＊ アメリカ ＊ 韓国

安紀子 ＊ （ペン） ＊ ロバート ＊ セーラ

（かばん） ＊ こんばんは ＊ さようなら ＊ こんにちは

何 ＊ か ＊ どこ ＊ （ドア）

Page 28: What's this?

1e, 2b, 3f, 4c, 5h, 6d, 7a, 8g

Page 30: Who orders what?

Customer 1: coffee & cake; Customer 2: black tea & sandwich; Customer 3: coffee & noodles; Customer 4: coffee & cake; Customer 5: black tea & pork cutlet

Page 31: Unscramble the conversation

g, a, e, c, f, h, d, b

Topic 4

Page 35: What does it mean?

Check your answers with the Key Words panel on page 34.

Page 35: What can you see?

レンジ	☑	ベッド	☑
冷蔵庫	☐	戸棚	☐
絵	☑	木	☐
コンピュータ	☑	猫	☑
テーブル	☑	椅子	☑
車	☐	本	☑
窓	☑	犬	☐
ペン	☑	かばん	☑
雑誌	☑	ネズミ	☐

Page 37: Which word?

1 前 ; 2 下 ; 3 上 ; 4 上 ; 5 となり ;
6 下 ; 7 中

Page 39: Where are the mice

There are many possible sentences.
If you can, check yours with a native speaker.

Page 41: True or False?

1 True; 2 False; 3 False; 4 False; 5 False; 6 True; 7 False;
8 True; 9 True; 10 True

Topic 5

Page 45: Can you remember?

Check your answers with the Key Words panel on page 44.

Page 46: What does it mean?

新しいソファー	*(a) new sofa*
小さいコーヒー	*(a) small coffee*
小さい犬	*(a) small dog*
とても古い車	*(a) very old car*
小さいネズミ	*(a) small mouse*
大きいサンドイッチ	*(a) big sandwich*
安い絵	*(a) cheap picture*
大きい木	*big trees*

Page 47: Listen and check

1 False; 2 True; 3 True; 4 False; 5 True

Page 47: Unscramble the sentences

1 c, a, b; 2 c, b, e, d, a; 3 c, d, a, b; 4 b, d, c, a

Page 50: Which word?

1 頭 ; 2 足 ; 3 お腹 ; 4 口 ; 5 指 ;
6 髪の毛 ; 7 耳 ; 8 鼻 ; 9 目 ; 10 腕

Page 51: At the pet show

この猫は毛がとても <u>6</u> です。 足も長い <u>2</u> 。
<u>1</u> が小さいです。

この犬 <u>4</u> 毛が短いです。 <u>3</u> がとても長いです。
目が <u>5</u> です。

Page 52: What does it look like?

There are many possible sentences.
If you can, check yours with a native speaker.

Topic 6

Page 55: Questions and answers

銀行はどこですか。	橋はあそこです。
レストランはありますか。	はい、レストランがあります。
ホテルはありますか。	公園は学校のとなりです。
公園はどこですか。	銀行は学校のとなりです。
橋はどこですか。	駅の前にホテルがあります。

Page 57: Word Square

car, boat, taxi, plane, bicycle, bus, train

駅	船	ラ	ソ	飛	行	機	ル
か	ば	ん	ス	レ	髪	港	ン
バ	公	で	さ	ビ	園	電	車
ー	タ	ク	シ	ー	フ	ク	す
こ	コ	ン	ピ	ュ	ー	タ	あ
レ	ー	毛	い	腹	テ	ら	そ
ト	バ	ス	う	の	な	車	こ
道	フ	ァ	自	転	車	子	シ

Page 60: Which way?

1 すみません、駅はどこですか。左に曲がって下さい。
　sumimasen, eki wa doko desu ka? hidari ni magatte kudasai.

2 すみません、バス停はどこですか。まっすぐ行って下さい。
　sumimasen, basutei wa doko desu ka? massugu itte kudasai.

3 すみません、駅はどこですか。右に曲がって下さい。
　sumimasen, eki wa doko desu ka? migi ni magatte kudasai.

4 すみません、銀行はどこですか。左に曲がって下さい。
　sumimasen, ginkou wa doko desu ka? hidari ni magatte kudasai.

5 すみません、博物館はどこですか。バスで行きます。
　sumimasen, hakubutsukan wa doko desu ka? basu de ikimasu.

6 すみません、空港はどこですか。電車で行きます。
　sumimasen, kuukou wa doko desu ka? densha de ikimasu.

Page 61: Around town

These are model answers. Yours may vary slightly.
the hotel
まっすぐ行って下さい。それから右に曲がって下さい。
ホテルは銀行のとなりです。 **massugu itte kudasai. sore kara
migi ni magatte kudasai. hoteru wa ginkou no tonari desu.**

the park
まっすぐ行って下さい。それから左に曲がって下さい。
公園は学校のとなりです。 **massugu itte kudasai. sore kara hidari ni magatte kudasai. kouen wa gakkou no tonari desu.**

the bus stop
まっすぐ行って下さい。それから左に曲がって下さい。
バス停は学校の前です。 **massugu itte kudasai. sore kara hidari ni magatte kudasai. basutei wa gakkou no mae desu.**

Page 62: Unscramble the conversation
e, c, a, b, d

Page 63: Game

Topic 7

Page 65: What does it mean?
Check your answers with the Key Words panel on page 64.

Page 67: Family Tree
There are many possible sentences.
If you can, check yours with a native speaker.

Page 68: Family Tree

Page 68: Questions and answers

Page 71: How many?

Page 71: Japanese sums
1 四 ; 2 六 ; 3 六 ; 4 八 ; 5 四 ;
6 十 ; 7 五 ; 8 九 ; 9 一

Topic 8

Page 75: What does it mean?
Check your answers with the Key Words panel on page 74.

Page 75: The tools of the trade

Page 77: Listen and note
1 *First name*: Akiko; *Family name*: Maruyama; *Nationality*: Japanese; *Spouse*: Shouji; *Children*: 2; *Occupation*: teacher

2 *First name*: Peter; *Family name*: Smith; *Nationality*: Irish; *Spouse*: Hannah; *Children*: 1; *Occupation*: accountant

Page 78: What does it mean?
1d, 2c, 3e, 4a, 5b

Page 78: Which word?
ハリーです。 3 です。
7 のメルボーンから来ました。
4 の名前はジュリー 6 。
1 が三人います。息子が 5
と 2 が二人います。

Page 80: Word Square

factory, university, bank, theatre, store, restaurant, hospital, office

事	工	場	ソ	テ	ー	ブ	ル
か	ば	ん	ス	病	髪	場	ン
さ	公	で	さ	院	園	車	場
お	店	空	劇	場	レ	銀	行
ご	大	学	ピ	ュ	ス	タ	あ
レ	ー	毛	い	腹	ト	事	そ
ト	院	誌	う	の	ラ	務	こ
ソ	フ	ァ	ー	場	ン	所	シ

Page 81: What are they saying?
1e, 2d, 3b, 4c, 5a, 6f

Page 82: Which word?
はじめまして。実です。東京 3 来ました。コックです。
ニューヨークの 7 に 1 。家族とニューヨークに住んで
います。 2 家族です。妻と 4 が二人います。妻は 6 です。
レストランのとなりに日本の学校があります。この 8 に勤
めています。娘はニューヨーク大学の 5 です。

Test Yourself

Page 84: May I have…?
Use … をお願いします… **o onegaishimasu** with the following:
1 コーヒー **koohi**; 2 お茶 **ocha**; 3 ケーキ **keeki**;
4 そば**soba**; 5 豚カツ **tonkatsu**; 6 サンドイッチ **sandoicchi**

Page 85: Listen and check
1 True; 2 False; 3 True; 4 False; 5 False; 6 False

Page 85: Which word?
はじめまして。亜紀子です。大阪から 6 。大
阪は 2 市です。私は 7 です。イギリスにあ
る日本の学校に 3 。 4 は医者です。
日本の学校のとなりに大きい病院があります。
夫はこの病院に勤めています。 1 が四人いま
す。 8 が三人と息子が 5 います。

Page 86: Read and check
1 True; 2 True; 3 False; 4 True; 5 False; 6 True; 7 True; 8 True

Page 87: Read and check
Check your answers with the Key Words panel on page 64.

Page 87: How do you say it?
1 夫は医者です。 **otto wa isha desu.**
2 妹がいます。 **imouto ga imasu.**
3 息子は技師です。 **musuko wa gishi desu.**
4 実さんは優子さんのお兄さんです。 **minoru san wa yuuko san no oniisan desu.**
5 妻の名前はセーラです。 **tsuma no namae wa seera desu.**
6 弟さんは俳優です。 **otoutosan wa haiyuu desu.**
7 子供はいません。 **kodomo wa imasen.**
8 娘が三人います。 **musume ga sannin imasu.**

Page 88: At the tourist office
さようなら **sayounara** *goodbye*
博物館 **hakubutsukan** *museum*
バス停 **basutei** *bus stop*
左に曲がって下さい **hidari ni magatte kudasai** *please turn left*
おはようございます **oyahou gozaimasu** *good morning*
どこ **doko** *where*
後ろ **ushiro** *behind*
ありがとうございます **arigatou gozaimasu** *thank you*
上 **ue** *on top of/above*
駅 **eki** *station*

Name cards:

✂

安紀子	優子	正	実
セーラ	ヘレン	メリー	リサ
ロバート	ピーター	ケン	マーク

Sentence-build cards:

✂

	こんにちは	さようなら	です
さん	何	お名前	か
？	は	ありがとうございます
。	こんばんは	おはようございます

Minoru	Tadashi	Yuuko	Akiko
Lisa	Mary	Helen	Sarah
Mark	Ken	Peter	Robert

I am	goodbye	hello	
(question marker)	name	what?	*"san"* (Mr., Mrs. etc.)
thank you		*(topic marker)*	?
good morning		good evening	.